Contents

What to Do 2

The Top of the Trees 4

Reaching the Top 6

A Walkway through the Trees 8

The Canopy Raft 10

Tower Cranes 12

Adventures in the Treetops 14

Something to Think About 16

Do You Need to Find an Answer? 18

Do You Want to Find Out More? 19

Word Help 20

Location Help 23

Index 24

What to Do

Choose a face

Remember the colour you have chosen.

When you see your face on the page, you are the LEADER.

The LEADER reads the text in the speech bubbles.

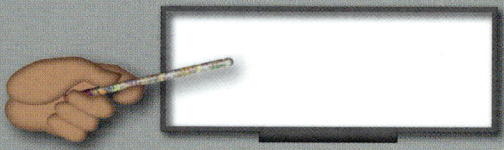

There are extra words and questions to help you on the teacher's whiteboard. The LEADER reads these aloud.

When you see this stop sign, the LEADER reads it aloud.

STOP
My predictions were right/wrong because . . .

You might need:

- to look at the WORD HELP on pages 20–22;
- to look at the LOCATION HELP on page 23;
- an atlas.

If you are the **LEADER**, follow these steps:

1 PREDICT

Think about what is on the page.

- Say to your group:

"I am looking at this page and I think it is going to be about . . ."

- Tell your group:

"Read the page to yourselves."

2 CLARIFY

Talk about words and their meaning.

- Say to your group:

"Are there any words you don't know?"

"Is there anything else on the page you didn't understand?"

- Talk about the words and their meanings with your group.
- Read the whiteboard.

- Ask your group to find the LET'S CHECK word in the WORD HELP on pages 20–22. Ask them to read the meaning of the word aloud.

3 ASK QUESTIONS

Talk about how to find out more.

- Say to your group:

"Who has a question about what we have read?"

- Question starters are: how..., why..., when..., where..., what..., who...
- Read the question on the whiteboard and talk about it with your group.

4 SUMMARISE

Think about who and what the story was mainly about.

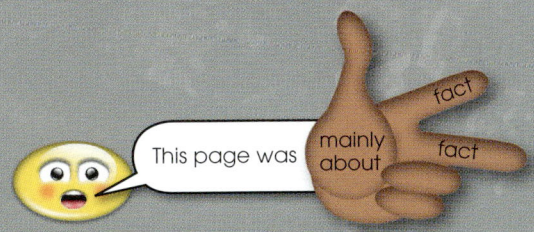

When you get to pages 16–17, you can talk to a partner or write and draw on your own.

 or

The Top of the Trees

In a **rainforest** there are tall trees. The top of these trees is called the **canopy**.

Scientists want to learn about the canopy. They want to learn about everything that lives there.

It is not easy to get to the top of these trees.

I am looking at this page and I think it is going to be about… because…

Are there any words you don't know?

Who has a question about what we have read?

Let's check:
rainforest

Why do you think it is not easy to get to the top of these trees?

Reaching the Top

I am looking at this page and I think it is going to be about… because…

Meg knows a lot about trees. She is sometimes called Canopy Meg.

Meg has always liked trees. When she was a child, she made tree houses. She **rescued** birds that had fallen from their nests.

Now, she has climbed to the tops of trees all over the world.

Are there any words you don't know?

Let's check: rescued

Who has a question about what we have read?

Why do you think Meg likes to climb to the top of trees?

A Walkway through the Trees

A **walkway** is like a **bridge**. It goes **between** the trees. A walkway is safe and it doesn't **harm** the trees.

Walkways in the rainforest were Meg's **idea**. Now, they are used by many people.

A walkway, however, cannot be made at the very top of the trees. The very top is where many scientists want to go.

I am looking at this page and I think it is going to be about… because…

Are there any words you don't know?

Who has a question about what we have read?

Let's check:
harm

Why do you think a walkway cannot be made at the top of the trees?

Meg and her son look at insects in the canopy.

This page was mainly about fact fact

STOP
My predictions were right/wrong because . . .

The Canopy Raft

I am looking at this page and I think it is going to be about… because…

Meg has **reached** the very top of the trees.

One way she loves to reach the top is by a **raft**. The raft is very light. It is filled with air. It has a huge net on it. A hot air balloon drops the raft onto the trees.

Scientists can stand on the raft and look into the trees.

Are there any words you don't know?

Let's check:
raft

Who has a question about what we have read?

Why do you think the raft needs to be light?

Tower Cranes

A **tower crane** is another way to get to the top. The crane can go up and down. It can go above the treetops. It can go all the way down to the ground, too.

Scientists are learning about life in the canopy. They know there are millions of insects. They have learned that these insects are eating the leaves.

I am looking at this page and I think it is going to be about… because…

Are there any words you don't know?

Who has a question about what we have read?

Let's check: crane

What do you think might be a problem if insects eat the leaves?

From a cage attached to the crane, scientists can reach the tree canopy.

This page was mainly about ___ fact fact

STOP
My predictions were right/wrong because . . .

Adventures in the Treetops

I am looking at this page and I think it is going to be about… because…

Meg and her sons have had many **adventures** in trees. They have slept in trees. They have even eaten insects.

Meg's job is to keep finding out more. She wants to help find the **secrets** of the treetops. There are still millions of animals that no one has seen. Many of them are in the treetops.

Are there any words you don't know?

Who has a question about what we have read?

Let's check:
adventures

What might you see, hear or feel if you slept in the trees?

Canopy Meg's sons get ready to go up into the canopy.

This page was mainly about ... fact fact

STOP
My predictions were right/wrong because . . .

Something to Think About

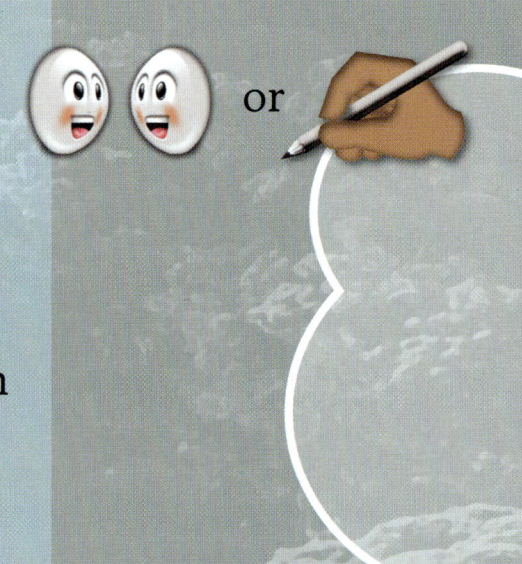 or

Think about the best way to reach the top of a tree. Talk about your ideas with a partner, or write them down.

Why?

The best way to reach the top is . . .

Do You Need to Find an Answer?

You could go to . . .

Library ❯

Expert ❯

Internet ❯

Do You Want to Find Out More?

You could look in books or on the internet. These key words could help you:

canopy

Canopy Meg

canopy raft

rainforest

rainforest walkways

Word Help

Dictionary

adventures	unusual and exciting experiences
between	in the middle of
bridge	something built to go over water, roads or railways
canopy	the top of the trees
crane	a tall machine used for lifting very heavy things
harm	to damage something or someone
idea	a thought or a plan
raft	a floating platform
rainforest	a wet, hot place with a lot of trees

reached	to get to somewhere
rescued	saved from being hurt
scientists	people who study or who know a lot about science
secrets	things not known
tower	a tall building
walkway	a path made by people

Word Help

Thesaurus

easy	simple
enormous	huge, mammoth, gigantic
harm	hurt
rescued	saved
secrets	mysteries
top	head, tip

Location Help

Where the Rainforests Are

■ Cool Rainforests

■ Warm Rainforests

Index

canopy 4–5, 9, 14

canopy raft 10–11

insects 9, 12, 14

rainforest 4, 7

scientists 4, 8, 10, 12–13

tower crane 12–13

walkway 8–9